MW01114050

This book belongs to:

____

Made in the USA
Middletown, DE
02 September 2023

37830497R00066